BUILDING CARDBOARD TOYS

Other books by the same author

DESIGNING HOUSES
Les Walker and Jeff Milstein
The Overlook Press
Woodstock, New York

A handbook for the laymen on the design of a personal
dwelling

BUILDING CARDBOARD DOLLHOUSES
Harper & Row, New York

5 Classic American House Designs
You Can Build Yourself

NEW ENGLAND COLONIAL DOLLHOUSE
Charles Scribner's Sons, New York

An easy-to-assemble dollhouse made of die-cut
white corrugated cardboard

BUILDING CARDBOARD TOYS

Written, photographed and illustrated by

Jeff Milstein

HARPER COLOPHON BOOKS
Harper & Row, Publishers
New York, Cambridge, Hagerstown, Philadelphia, San Francisco
London, Mexico City, São Paulo, Sydney

BUILDING CARDBOARD TOYS. Copyright ©1979 by Jeffrey Milstein. All rights reserved. Printed in the United States of America. No part of this book may be used or reproduced in any manner without written permission except in the case of brief quotations embodied in critical articles and reviews. For information address Harper & Row, Publishers, Inc., 10 East 53rd Street, New York, N.Y. 10022. Published simultaneously in Canada by Fitzhenry & Whiteside Limited, Toronto.

First HARPER COLOPHON edition published 1979

LIBRARY OF CONGRESS CATALOG NUMBER: 79-2027
ISBN: 0-06-090666-9

79 80 81 82 83 10 9 8 7 6 5 4 3 2 1

Contents

Introduction

Every day our mechanized society discards tons of corrugated cardboard that was used for shipping packages. This can be seen in piles that gather around the aisles in supermarkets, or fill up the back rooms of most any retail store. This book is intended to show you how to take this discarded corrugated and recycle it into sturdy colorful toys. Corrugated is fun and easy to work with. You don't need expensive tools or a workshop; there is none of the dust and noise created when working with wood. While corrugated is not as strong as wood, it is a simple matter to cut a replacement part, should the plane have a bad landing.

The first chapter describes what tools and materials you will need and tells where to find them. The second chapter shows you how to build. By following the easy step-by-step methods shown, you will learn how to draw the plan, and how to cut, score, fold, curve, glue, and paint the cardboard so you can create toys from the plans included in the book or of your own design. The third chapter includes detailed plans for five toys: A racer, a dump truck, a steamship, an airplane, and a locomotive. They vary in difficulty, the racer being the easiest and the locomotive the most difficult. Each toy is shown with exploded assembly drawings and photographs.

The finished toys are great fun to look at, play with, and give as gifts, but the most fun is building them.

Chapter 1
GATHERING SUPPLIES

One of the advantages of building toys out of corrugated cardboard is that you don't need much in the way of tools and materials. Here is what you need, and where to find it.

Materials

1 Corrugated Cardboard

Corrugated cardboard is the basic building material. In its most common form it is made up of 3 pieces of paper. The middle piece, which is corrugated, is glued at the ridges to the top and bottom papers. The corrugated center acts like the web of a beam, giving the cardboard its strength.

If you can scavenge a bit you can get it free. Supermarkets, drugstores, liquor and hardware stores are good bets. Store managers are usually delighted to get empty cartons off their hands. Appliance and furniture stores are good for big pieces.

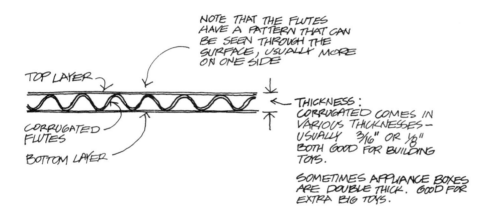

NOTE THAT THE FLUTES HAVE A PATTERN THAT CAN BE SEEN THROUGH THE SURFACE, USUALLY MORE ON ONE SIDE

TOP LAYER

CORRUGATED FLUTES

BOTTOM LAYER

THICKNESS: CORRUGATED COMES IN VARIOUS THICKNESSES — USUALLY 3/16" OR 1/8" BOTH GOOD FOR BUILDING TOYS.

SOMETIMES APPLIANCE BOXES ARE DOUBLE THICK. GOOD FOR EXTRA BIG TOYS.

2 Chipboard

This is an inexpensive solid cardboard. You can find it in laundered shirts, shoe boxes, gift boxes and the bottoms of paper pads. It comes in several different thicknesses. If it has a smooth paper finish it is called poster board. A big piece of heavy chipboard makes a good cutting board for cutting out corrugated cardboard.

3 Dowels

1/4″ wood dowels are used for wheel axles. You can find them at hardware or hobby shops.

HARDWOOD DOWEL

¼″

4 Paint & Glue Supplies

Here are the paint and glue supplies you will need. You should be able to find anything you don't already have at the hardware store.

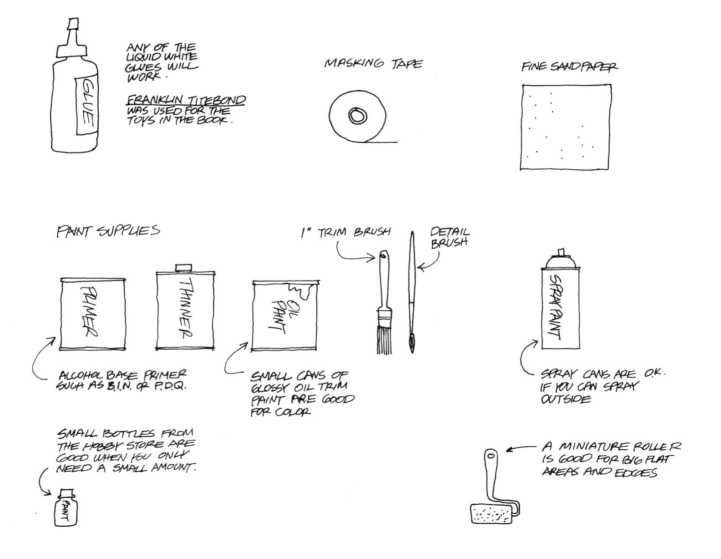

ANY OF THE LIQUID WHITE GLUES WILL WORK.

FRANKLIN TITEBOND WAS USED FOR THE TOYS IN THE BOOK.

MASKING TAPE

FINE SANDPAPER

PAINT SUPPLIES

1" TRIM BRUSH

DETAIL BRUSH

ALCOHOL BASE PRIMER SUCH AS B.I.N. OR P.D.Q.

SMALL CANS OF GLOSSY OIL TRIM PAINT ARE GOOD FOR COLOR

SPRAY CANS ARE O.K. IF YOU CAN SPRAY OUTSIDE

SMALL BOTTLES FROM THE HOBBY STORE ARE GOOD WHEN YOU ONLY NEED A SMALL AMOUNT.

A MINIATURE ROLLER IS GOOD FOR BIG FLAT AREAS AND EDGES

Tools

Here are the basic tools you will need. You should be able to find anything you need at an art supply or stationery store.

UTILITY KNIFE

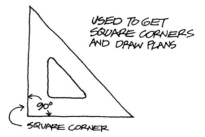

A DIME OPENS KNIFE TO REPLACE BLADES

GET EXTRA BLADES

METAL STRAIGHT EDGE

A HEAVY ONE IS BEST. USED FOR CUTTING STRAIGHT LINES AND MEASURING

DRAFTING TRIANGLE

USED TO GET SQUARE CORNERS AND DRAW PLANS

90°

SQUARE CORNER

SCISSORS

CAN BE USED TO CUT THIN CORRUGATED & CHIPBOARD

COMPASS   PAPER PUNCH ¼" HOLE

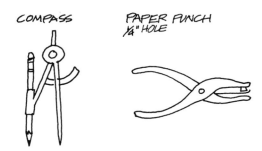

CIRCLE CUTTER   X-ACTO # 7754

CAN BE MAIL ORDERED FROM CHARRETTE 212 E. 54th ST., N.Y., N.Y. $ 7.50 + SHPG. ITEM 32-7254

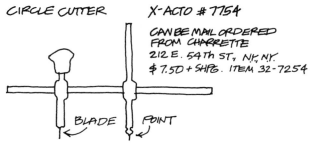

BLADE   POINT

FOR THE SERIOUS BUILDER X-ACTO MAKES A BEAM COMPASS & CIRCLE CUTTER WHICH YOU CAN USE TO CUT NEAT CIRCLES

Chapter 2
BUILDING YOUR TOYS

This chapter shows you how to build your toys. Study the techniques and practice them on some cardboard scraps. Take your time and work carefully, particularly when working with sharp tools.

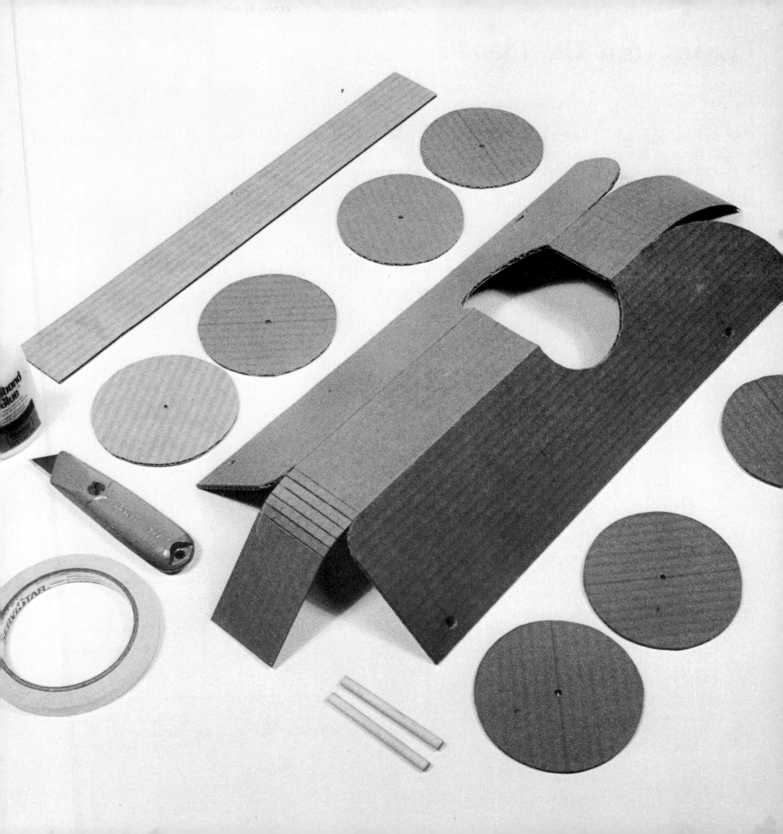

Laying out the Plans

The first step is to have a plan for your toy. You can use one from the book or you can design your own. The plan has to be drawn on the cardboard so it can be cut out.

First, square up a piece of cardboard, using the square angle of the triangle. Then locate key points along the edges and connect these with light lines. Use these lines to locate other lines, axle centers, curves, score lines, etc. Then go back and darken in the shapes to be cut out. Keep your pencil sharp and an eraser handy.

For example, suppose you wanted to lay out the plan for the racer. Here is how you would do it:

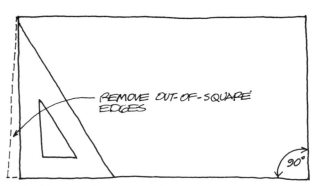

REMOVE OUT-OF-SQUARE EDGES

90°

1. GET A PIECE OF CORRUGATED BIG ENOUGH FOR THE PART. SQUARE UP THE CORNERS WITH THE TRIANGLE.

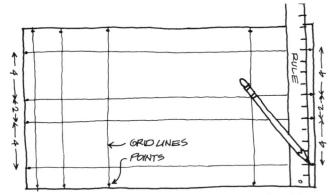

GRID LINES
POINTS
RULE

2. LOCATE PRIMARY DIMENSION POINTS ALONG THE SIDES AND TOP AS SHOWN. THEN CONNECT THE POINTS WITH LIGHT LINES TO MAKE A PLAN GRID.

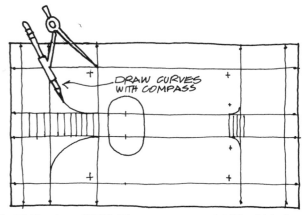

DRAW CURVES WITH COMPASS

3. USE THE GRID TO LOCATE CURVES, AXLE HOLES AND OTHER LINES.

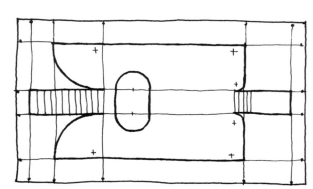

4. GO BACK AND DARKEN THE LINES TO BE CUT. NOW YOU ARE READY TO CUT OUT THE SHAPE.

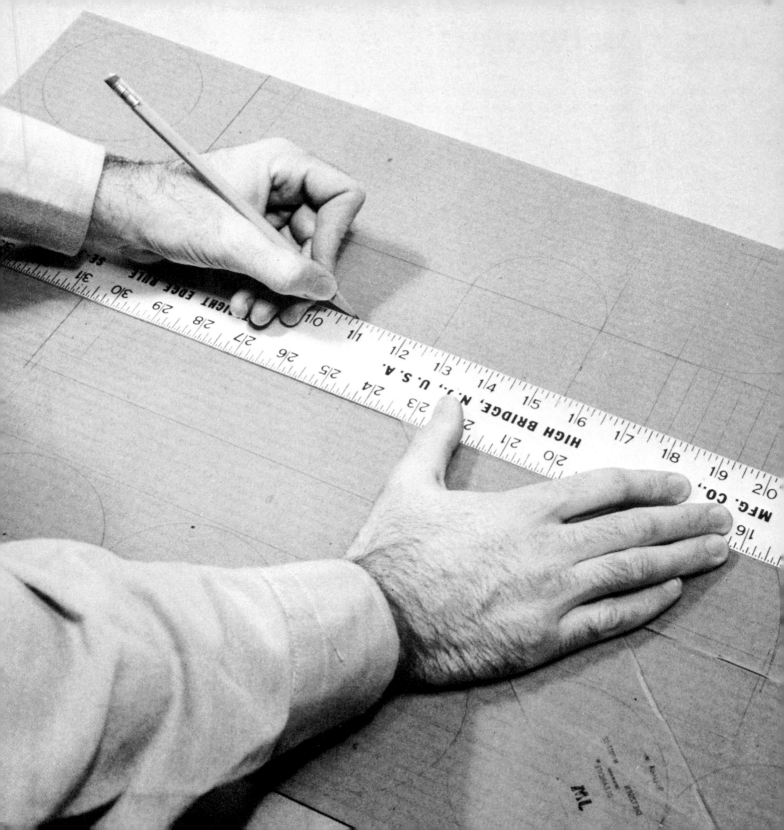

Transferring Patterns

Some parts of the plans in the book are shown as full size patterns to be transferred to the cardboard. Suppose you wanted to transfer the number 8 to the racer for painting. Here is how to do that.

TRACE THE NUMBER OUT OF THE BOOK.

TURN TRACING PAPER OVER, BLACKEN BACK WITH SOFT PENCIL.

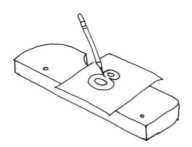

RE-TRACE NUMBER, TRANSFERING CARBON FROM BACK OF NUMBER

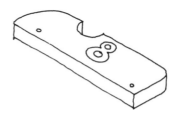

NOW YOU HAVE THE PATTERN TRANSFERRED

Grids

Some parts are shown on the plans using a scaled down grid. Each square on the scaled down grid represents a one inch square. What you do is draw a one inch grid on the cardboard. Locate the points where the curve crosses the grid by comparing the scaled down grid to the one inch grid. Then just connect the dots. For example, here is how you would draw the curve from the plan of the airplane:

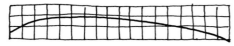

1. FOR EXAMPLE, IF THIS WERE THE PLAN TO BE DRAWN

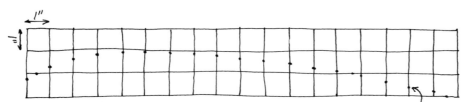

2. DRAW A SIMILAR GRID USING 1" SQUARES. MAKE DOTS IN PLACES WHERE CURVE INTERSECTS GRID.

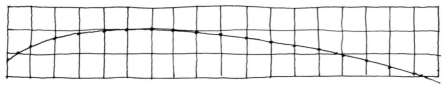

3. DRAW A SMOOTH CURVE BETWEEN THE DOTS.

19

Cutting out the Pieces

Here are some pointers that will help you to cut out the pieces you have drawn up. Place the cardboard to be cut on a piece of heavy chipboard or smooth plywood cutting board. If the cutting board surface is rough, you will find that the bottom of the cardboard tears as the cut is made. Tearing is also a sign that the blade is dull. Draw the blade across the surface the first time pressing moderately, cutting the top surface. Then repeat the cut. The blade will want to stay in the slot you made on the first cut. 2 or 3 draws, depending on the blade condition, will cut the piece.

Cutting out curved shapes is not too difficult if you just go slowly along the line, making several passes for each cut, without trying to cut too deeply at once. On thin cardboard you can use a pair of scissors.

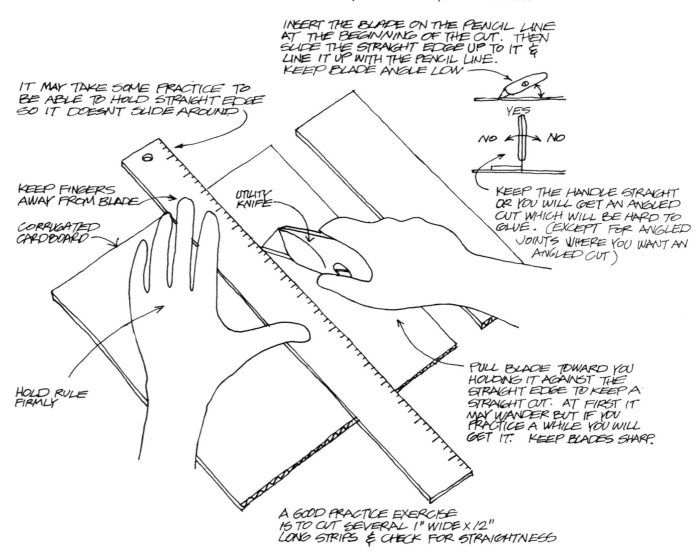

INSERT THE BLADE ON THE PENCIL LINE AT THE BEGINNING OF THE CUT. THEN SLIDE THE STRAIGHT EDGE UP TO IT & LINE IT UP WITH THE PENCIL LINE. KEEP BLADE ANGLE LOW

YES

NO ← → NO

KEEP THE HANDLE STRAIGHT OR YOU WILL GET AN ANGLED CUT WHICH WILL BE HARD TO GLUE. (EXCEPT FOR ANGLED JOINTS WHERE YOU WANT AN ANGLED CUT)

IT MAY TAKE SOME PRACTICE TO BE ABLE TO HOLD STRAIGHT EDGE SO IT DOESN'T SLIDE AROUND

KEEP FINGERS AWAY FROM BLADE

CORRUGATED CARDBOARD

UTILITY KNIFE

HOLD RULE FIRMLY

PULL BLADE TOWARD YOU HOLDING IT AGAINST THE STRAIGHT EDGE TO KEEP A STRAIGHT CUT. AT FIRST IT MAY WANDER BUT IF YOU PRACTICE A WHILE YOU WILL GET IT. KEEP BLADES SHARP.

A GOOD PRACTICE EXERCISE IS TO CUT SEVERAL 1" WIDE x 12" LONG STRIPS & CHECK FOR STRAIGHTNESS

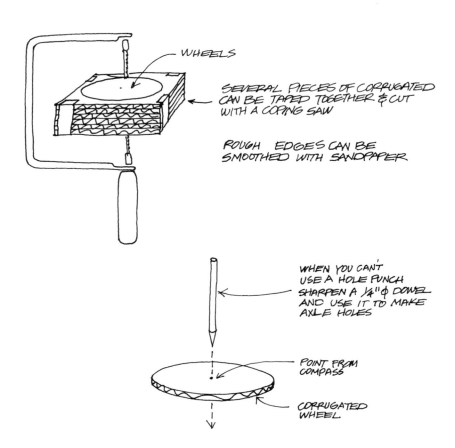

WHEELS

SEVERAL PIECES OF CORRUGATED CAN BE TAPED TOGETHER & CUT WITH A COPING SAW

ROUGH EDGES CAN BE SMOOTHED WITH SANDPAPER

WHEN YOU CAN'T USE A HOLE PUNCH SHARPEN A 1/4"∅ DOWEL AND USE IT TO MAKE AXLE HOLES

POINT FROM COMPASS

CORRUGATED WHEEL

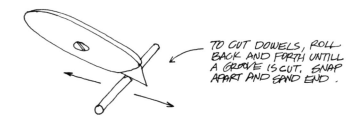

TO CUT DOWELS, ROLL BACK AND FORTH UNTILL A GROOVE IS CUT. SNAP APART AND SAND END.

Making a Mitred Corner

Here is how to make a neat corner glue joint that doesn't show the corrugations.

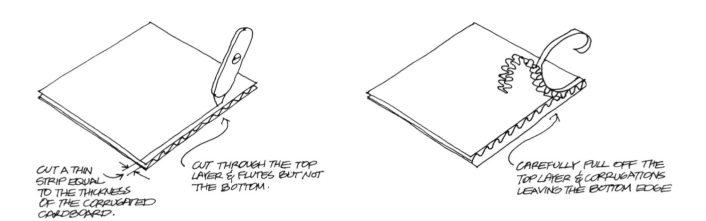

CUT A THIN STRIP EQUAL TO THE THICKNESS OF THE CORRUGATED CARDBOARD.

CUT THROUGH THE TOP LAYER & FLUTES BUT NOT THE BOTTOM.

CAREFULLY PULL OFF THE TOP LAYER & CORRUGATIONS LEAVING THE BOTTOM EDGE

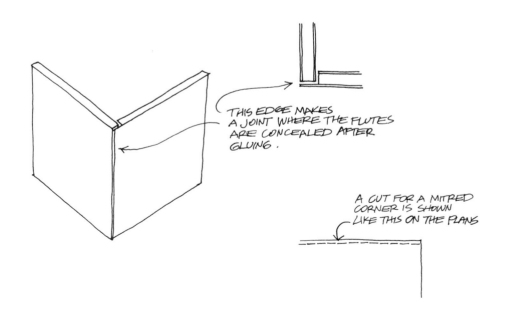

THIS EDGE MAKES A JOINT WHERE THE FLUTES ARE CONCEALED AFTER GLUING.

A CUT FOR A MITRED CORNER IS SHOWN LIKE THIS ON THE PLANS

Scoring & Folding

Whenever possible joints should be scored and folded rather than glued. It gives a neater joint and makes construction easier. Always be sure to score and crush the corrugations on the side that will be inside the fold.

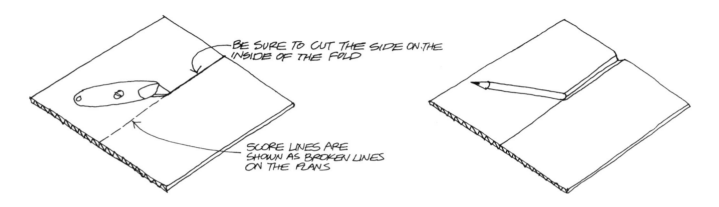

BE SURE TO CUT THE SIDE ON THE INSIDE OF THE FOLD

SCORE LINES ARE SHOWN AS BROKEN LINES ON THE PLANS

a CUT THROUGH TOP SIDE & CORRUGATIONS BUT BE CAREFUL NOT TO CUT THROUGH BOTTOM PAPER. PRACTICE A FEW.

b PULL THE ROUND END OF A PENCIL ACROSS THE CUT SEVERAL TIMES CRUSHING THE CORRUGATIONS.

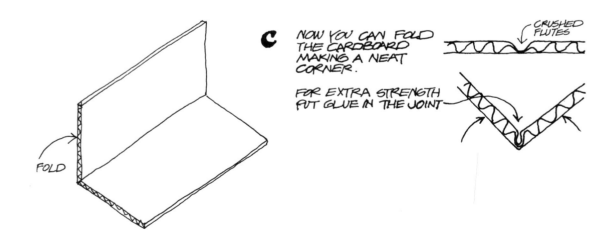

c NOW YOU CAN FOLD THE CARDBOARD MAKING A NEAT CORNER.

FOR EXTRA STRENGTH PUT GLUE IN THE JOINT

CRUSHED FLUTES

FOLD

Curving Corrugated

You can make neat curved shapes out of corrugated cardboard by carefully scoring the cardboard on one side with neat, evenly spaced cuts as shown below.

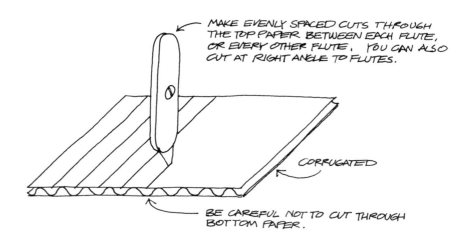

MAKE EVENLY SPACED CUTS THROUGH THE TOP PAPER BETWEEN EACH FLUTE, OR EVERY OTHER FLUTE. YOU CAN ALSO CUT AT RIGHT ANGLE TO FLUTES.

CORRUGATED

BE CAREFUL NOT TO CUT THROUGH BOTTOM PAPER.

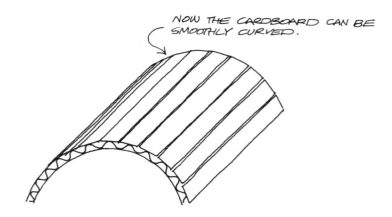

NOW THE CARDBOARD CAN BE SMOOTHLY CURVED.

Making a Tube

If you can't find the size tube you want inside a roll of some household item you can make your own. Here's how.

KEEPING A PIECE OF HEAVY PAPER TAUT, PULL IT ACROSS THE EDGE OF A TABLE.

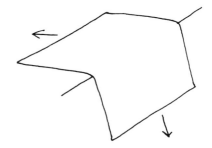

THIS WILL CURVE THE PAPER

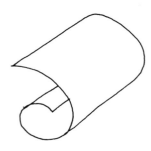

ROLL THE PAPER INTO A TIGHT TUBE THE DESIRED DIAMETER AND APPLY GLUE TO THE EDGE

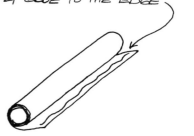

USE A DAMP RAG OR SPONGE TO CLEAN THE JOINT

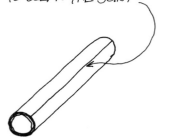

Assembling the Pieces

Here are some tips that will help you in assembling the pieces.

BEFORE GLUING THE PIECES CHECK THAT THE EDGES ARE STRAIGHT & SQUARE. IF THE CUTS ARE ANGLED AS SHOWN HERE THEY WON'T MAKE GOOD CONTACT FOR GLUING

USE A PIECE OF SANDPAPER WRAPPED AROUND A WOOD BLOCK TO SQUARE UP BAD CUTS THAT WILL BE GLUE JOINTS.

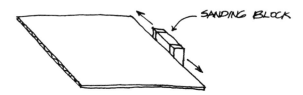

SANDING BLOCK

APPLYING GLUE:

APPLY GLUE TO BOTH PIECES TO BE GLUED. SQUEEZE THE BOTTLE WHILE PULLING IT ALONG THE EDGE. RUN YOUR FINGER LIGHTLY OVER THE BEAD TO SPREAD IT OUT. ON THE FLAT SIDE.

GLUE BEAD

FINGER.

ON THE NARROW EDGE RUB THE NOZZLE BACK & FORTH TO APPLY THE GLUE. TAP FINGER ALONG THE EDGE TO SPREAD OUT

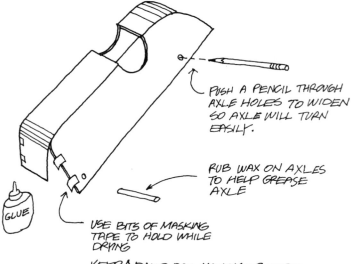

PUSH A PENCIL THROUGH AXLE HOLES TO WIDEN SO AXLE WILL TURN EASILY.

RUB WAX ON AXLES TO HELP GREASE AXLE

GLUE

USE BITS OF MASKING TAPE TO HOLD WHILE DRYING

KEEP A DAMP RAG HANDY TO WIPE AWAY EXCESS GLUE.

Painting

The key to a good paint job is the undercoat. You must first prime corrugated cardboard with an alcohol base, quick-drying primer such as B.I.N. or P.D.Q. This is absolutely necessary; otherwise the cardboard will absorb the paint and give a poor finish. A small roller is an excellent way to apply primer and paint. Spray paint is good, especially for small pieces. But if you spray, be sure to do it outside, where you can avoid inhaling the vapors. Once the surface is primed, you can use either oil or latex paint. Oil will give a brighter, stronger finish but latex is less messy and has no odor, making it more suitable for small children.

Painting your toys with oil will give them added strength.

If you don't find the colors you want, try mixing your own.

While some parts are easier to paint before assembly, often is is better to paint after assembly since glue holds better to unpainted cardboard. If you do have to glue painted surfaces, roughen first with sandpaper.

Chapter 3
PLANS For 5 TOYS

This chapter contains plans and assembly instructions for five toys. The racer is the easiest to build and the locomotive the most difficult. If you have studied Chapter 2 and practiced the techniques, you shouldn't have any trouble building.

You can use the colors shown on the cover as a guide for painting or you can choose your own colors.

Notes for the Plans

Here are some notes and symbols that will help you to read the plans.

The plans are drawn to a scale of 1/4" equals 1" except for the parts which are shown as full size patterns.

Parts that are symmetrical are only dimensioned on one side.

The numbers are dimensions in inches, based on 1/8" thick corrugated. If thicker or thinner cardboard is used you may have to slightly adjust some dimensions.

Except where noted the cardboard to be used is corrugated. When it is important that the corrutaged flutes run in a particular direction, several short lines will represent the flutes: ≡

A score line to be cut partially through the cardboard, for curving, is shown by a broken line: — — — —

A score-fold line to be folded is shown by a broken line with a fold note: — FOLD — —

The removal of a thin strip of corrugated for a mitred corner is shown by a dotted line close to the edge: ========

The small circles represent axle holes and should be made with a 1/4" hole punch if possible: —⊙— o

The radius of a curve is shown as an arrow with a number showing the radius in inches:

1 Racer

Plans

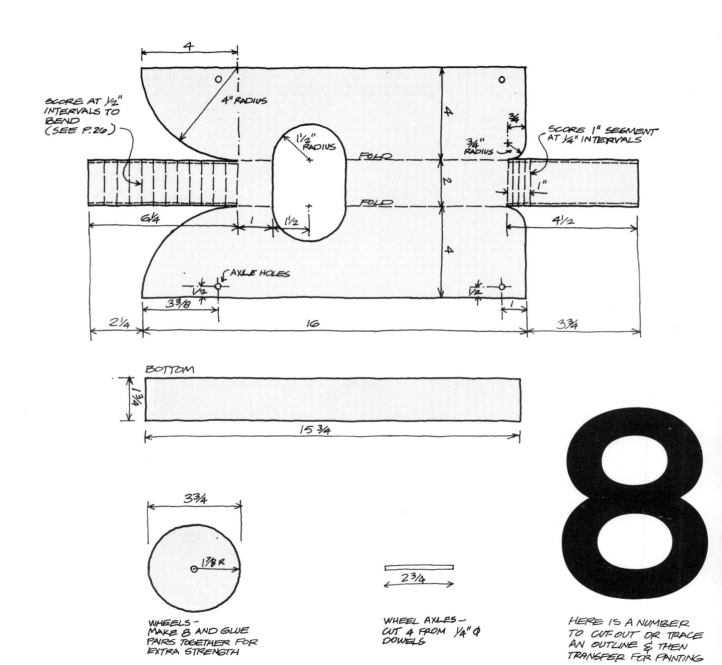

4

SCORE AT 1/2"
INTERVALS TO
BEND
(SEE P.26)

4" RADIUS

1 1/2" RADIUS

FOLD

3/4

3/4" RADIUS

SCORE 1" SEGMENT
AT 1/4" INTERVALS

1"

FOLD

4

2

4

6 1/4

1

1 1/2

4 1/2

AXLE HOLES

1/2

3 3/8

1/2

1

2 1/4

16

3 3/4

BOTTOM

1 3/4

15 3/4

3 3/4

1 7/8 R

WHEELS —
MAKE 8 AND GLUE
PAIRS TOGETHER FOR
EXTRA STRENGTH

2 3/4

WHEEL AXLES —
CUT 4 FROM 1/4" Φ
DOWELS

HERE IS A NUMBER
TO CUT-OUT OR TRACE
AN OUTLINE & THEN
TRANSFER FOR PAINTING

Assembly

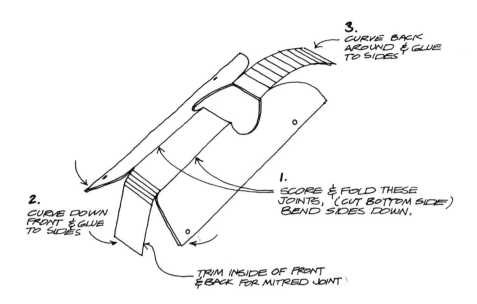

3. CURVE BACK AROUND & GLUE TO SIDES

1. SCORE & FOLD THESE JOINTS, (CUT BOTTOM SIDE) BEND SIDES DOWN.

2. CURVE DOWN FRONT & GLUE TO SIDES

TRIM INSIDE OF FRONT & BACK FOR MITRED JOINT

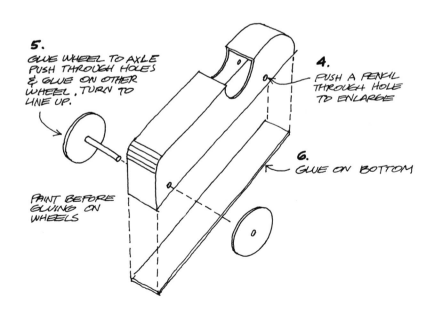

5. GLUE WHEEL TO AXLE PUSH THROUGH HOLES & GLUE ON OTHER WHEEL. TURN TO LINE UP.

4. PUSH A PENCIL THROUGH HOLE TO ENLARGE

6. GLUE ON BOTTOM

PAINT BEFORE GLUING ON WHEELS

2 Steamship

Plans

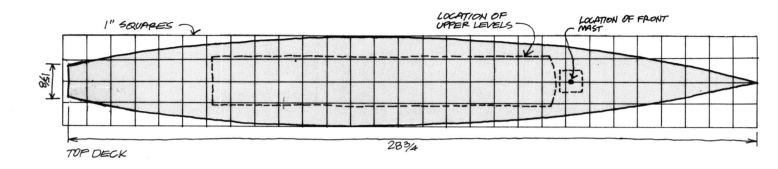

1" SQUARES

LOCATION OF UPPER LEVELS

LOCATION OF FRONT MAST

1⅝

TOP DECK

28¾

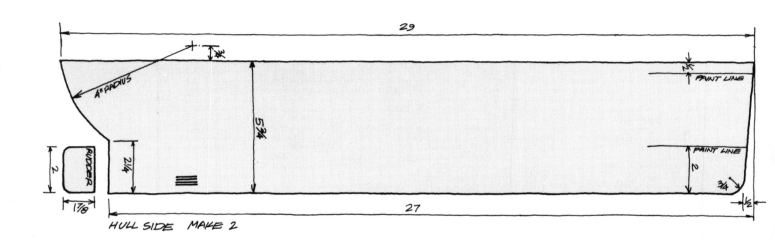

29

⅜

4" RADIUS

5¾

RUDDER

2

2¼

2

PAINT LINE

PAINT LINE

¾

½

1⅞

HULL SIDE   MAKE 2

27

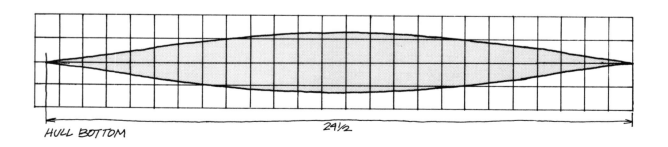

HULL BOTTOM

24½

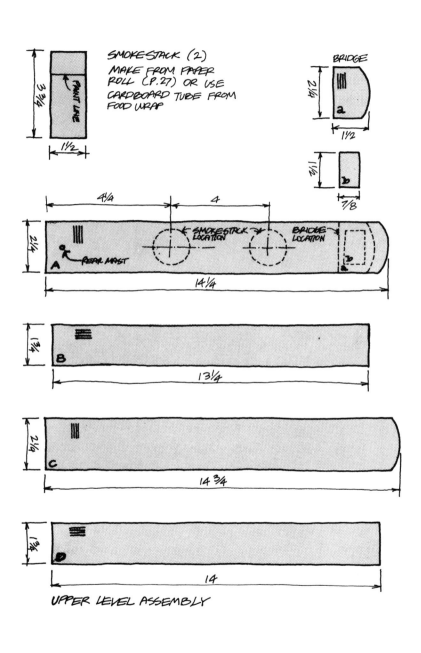

SMOKESTACK (2)
MAKE FROM PAPER
ROLL (P.27) OR USE
CARDBOARD TUBE FROM
FOOD WRAP

PRINT LINE

3 3/4

1 1/2

BRIDGE

2 1/4

a

1 1/2

1 1/2

b

7/8

4 1/4

4

SMOKESTACK
LOCATION

BRIDGE
LOCATION

2 1/4

A

REAR MAST

b

14 1/4

1 3/4

B

13 1/4

2 1/4

C

14 3/4

1 3/4

D

14

UPPER LEVEL ASSEMBLY

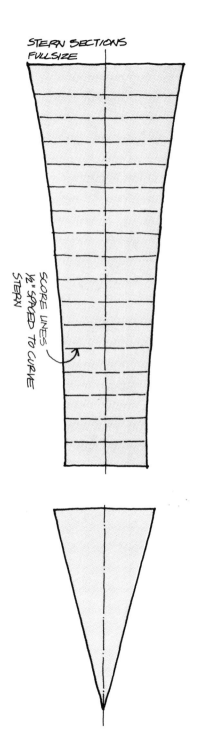

STERN SECTIONS
FULLSIZE

SCORE LINES
1/2" SPACED TO CURVE
STERN

Assembly

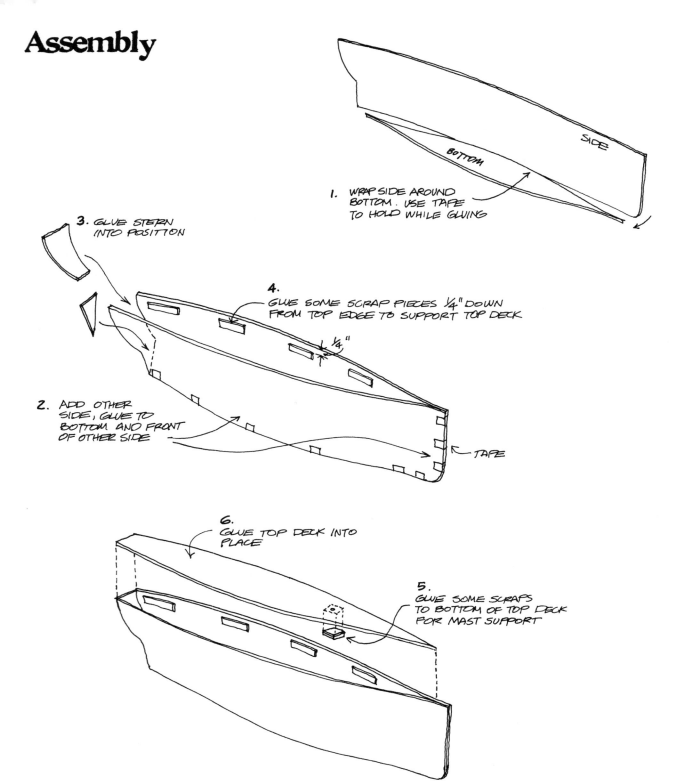

1. WRAP SIDE AROUND BOTTOM. USE TAPE TO HOLD WHILE GLUING

SIDE

BOTTOM

3. GLUE STERN INTO POSITION

4. GLUE SOME SCRAP PIECES 1/4" DOWN FROM TOP EDGE TO SUPPORT TOP DECK

1/4"

2. ADD OTHER SIDE, GLUE TO BOTTOM AND FRONT OF OTHER SIDE

TAPE

6. GLUE TOP DECK INTO PLACE

5. GLUE SOME SCRAPS TO BOTTOM OF TOP DECK FOR MAST SUPPORT

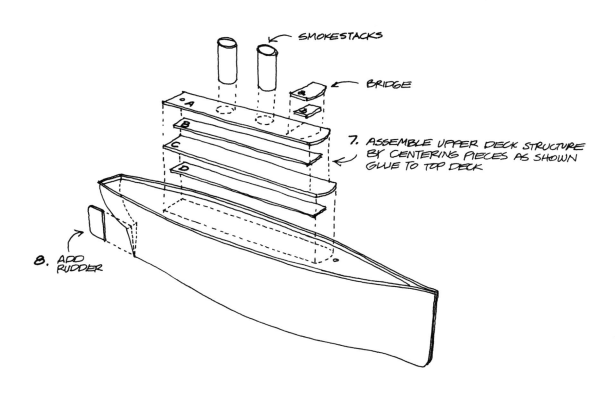

SMOKESTACKS

BRIDGE

7. ASSEMBLE UPPER DECK STRUCTURE BY CENTERING PIECES AS SHOWN GLUE TO TOP DECK

A
B
C
D

8. ADD RUDDER

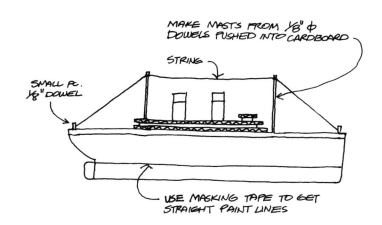

MAKE MASTS FROM ⅛" φ DOWELS PUSHED INTO CARDBOARD

STRING

SMALL PC. ⅛" DOWEL

USE MASKING TAPE TO GET STRAIGHT PAINT LINES

3 Dump Truck

Plans

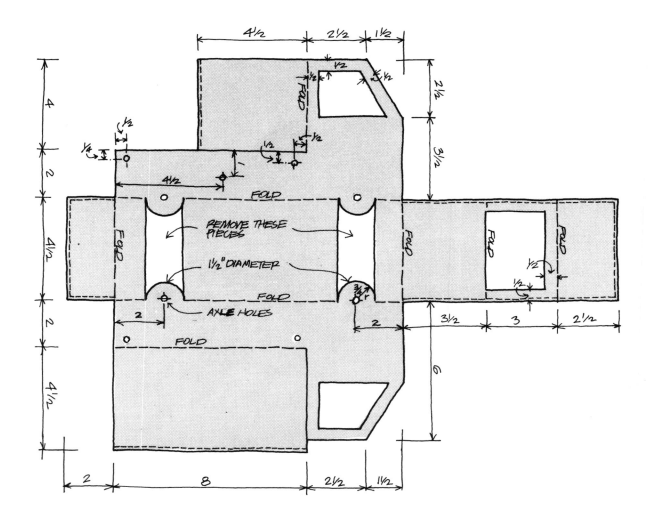

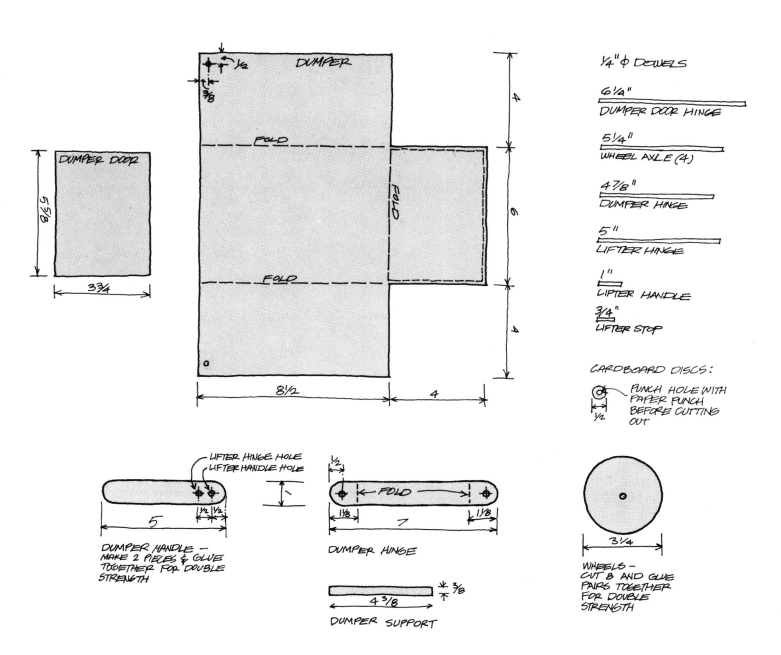

Assembly

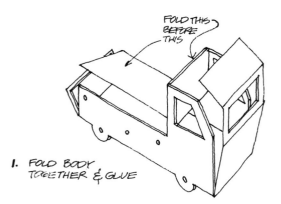

1. FOLD BODY TOGETHER & GLUE

FOLD THIS BEFORE THIS

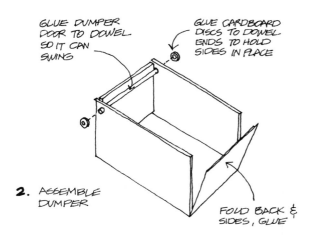

GLUE DUMPER DOOR TO DOWEL SO IT CAN SWING

GLUE CARDBOARD DISCS TO DOWEL ENDS TO HOLD SIDES IN PLACE

2. ASSEMBLE DUMPER

FOLD BACK & SIDES, GLUE

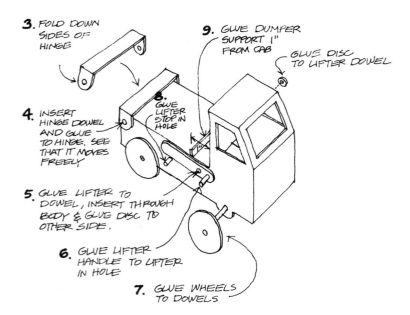

3. FOLD DOWN SIDES OF HINGE

9. GLUE DUMPER SUPPORT 1" FROM CAB

GLUE DISC TO LIFTER DOWEL

8. GLUE LIFTER STOP IN HOLE

4. INSERT HINGE DOWEL AND GLUE TO HINGE. SEE THAT IT MOVES FREELY

5. GLUE LIFTER TO DOWEL, INSERT THROUGH BODY & GLUE DISC TO OTHER SIDE.

6. GLUE LIFTER HANDLE TO LIFTER IN HOLE

7. GLUE WHEELS TO DOWELS

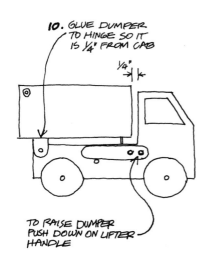

10. GLUE DUMPER TO HINGE SO IT IS ¼" FROM CAB

¼"

TO RAISE DUMPER PUSH DOWN ON LIFTER HANDLE

4 Airplane

Plans

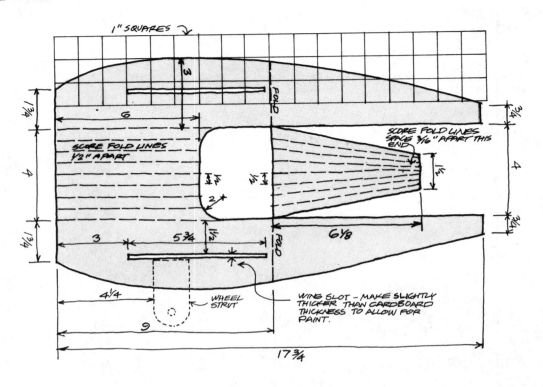

1" SQUARES

3

1/4

6

SCORE FOLD LINES 1/2" APART

4

SCORE FOLD LINES SPACE 3/16" APART THIS END

3/4

4

3/4

1/2

1/2

2

FOLD

1 1/2

6 1/8

1 3/4

3

5 3/4

1 1/2

FOLD

WHEEL STRUT

WING SLOT - MAKE SLIGHTLY THICKER THAN CARDBOARD THICKNESS TO ALLOW FOR PAINT.

4 1/4

9

17 3/4

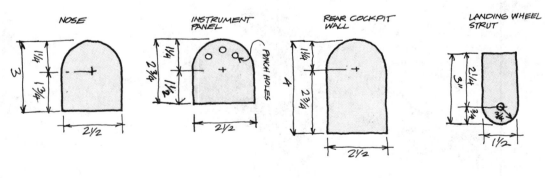

NOSE
3
1 1/4
1 3/4
2 1/2

INSTRUMENT PANEL
2 3/4
1 1/4
1 1/2
PINCH HOLES
2 1/2

REAR COCKPIT WALL
1 1/4
4
2 3/4
2 1/2

LANDING WHEEL STRUT
3"
2 1/4
3/4
1 1/2

BOTTOM - CUT FROM THIN CHIP OR POSTER BOARD

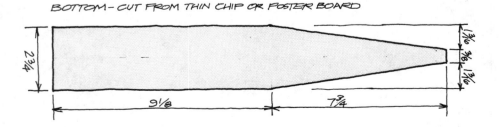

2 3/4

9 1/8

7 3/4

1 3/16
3/16
1 3/16

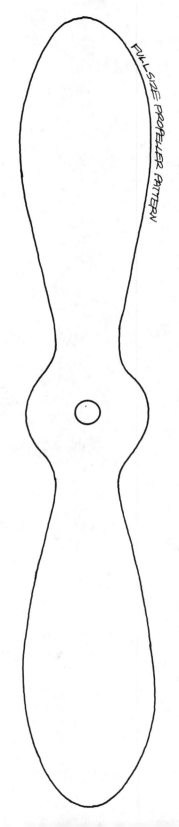

FULL-SIZE PROPELLER PATTERN

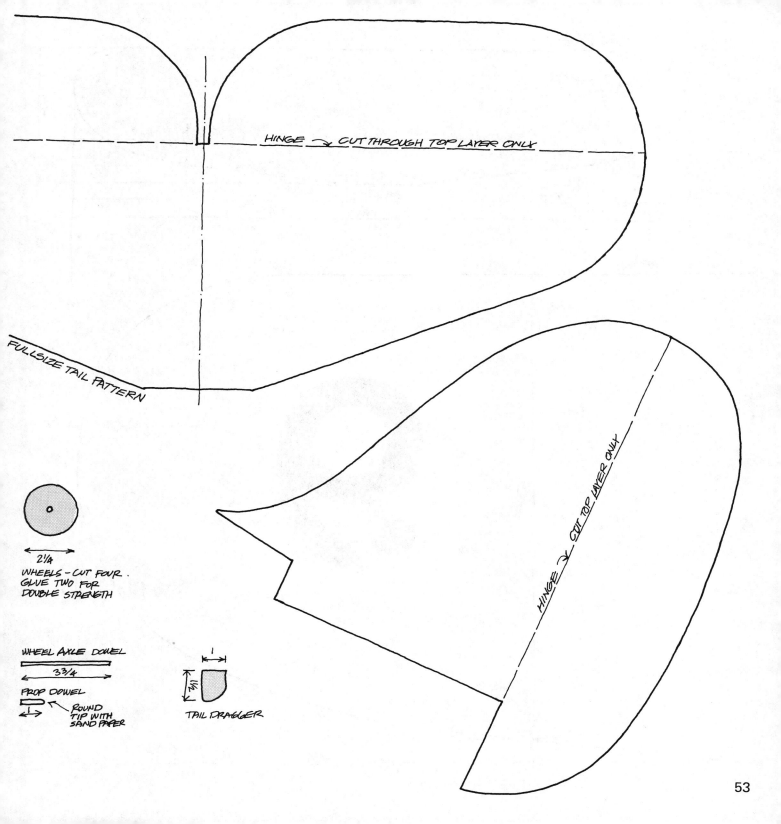

HINGE → CUT THROUGH TOP LAYER ONLY

FULLSIZE TAIL PATTERN

2¼

WHEELS – CUT FOUR.
GLUE TWO FOR
DOUBLE STRENGTH

WHEEL AXLE DOWEL

3¾

PROP DOWEL

ROUND
TIP WITH
SAND PAPER

1

11/16

TAIL DRAGGER

HINGE → CUT TOP LAYER ONLY

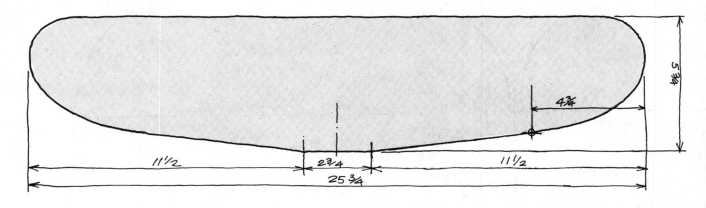

FULLSIZE WING TIP

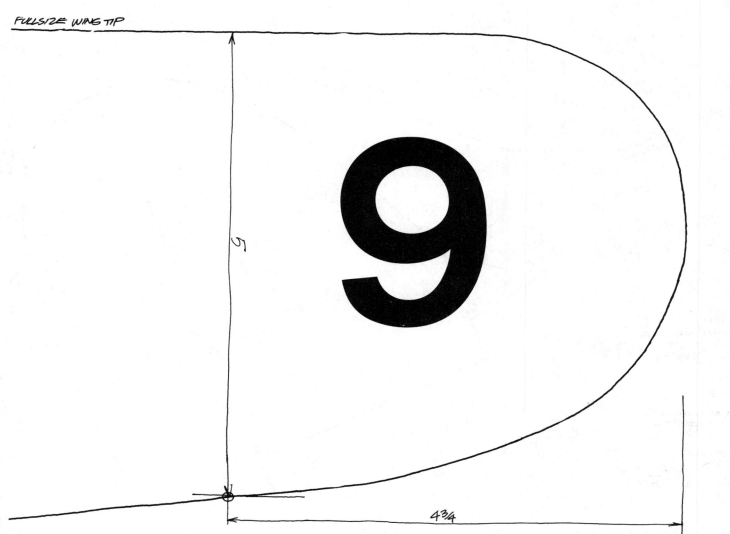

Assembly

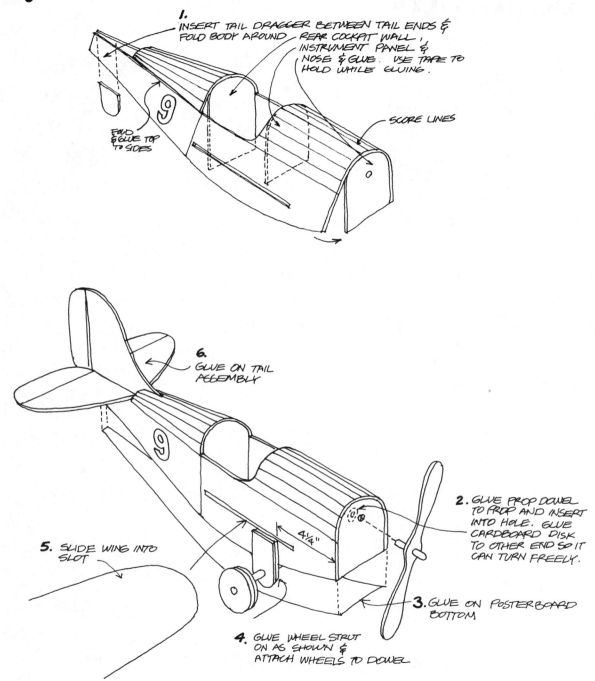

1. INSERT TAIL DRAGGER BETWEEN TAIL ENDS & FOLD BODY AROUND REAR COCKPIT WALL, INSTRUMENT PANEL & NOSE & GLUE. USE TAPE TO HOLD WHILE GLUING.

SCORE LINES

FOLD & GLUE TOP TO SIDES

6. GLUE ON TAIL ASSEMBLY

2. GLUE PROP DOWEL TO PROP AND INSERT INTO HOLE. GLUE CARDBOARD DISK TO OTHER END SO IT CAN TURN FREELY.

3. GLUE ON POSTERBOARD BOTTOM

4. GLUE WHEEL STRUT ON AS SHOWN & ATTACH WHEELS TO DOWEL

5. SLIDE WING INTO SLOT

4¼"

5 Locomotive

Plans

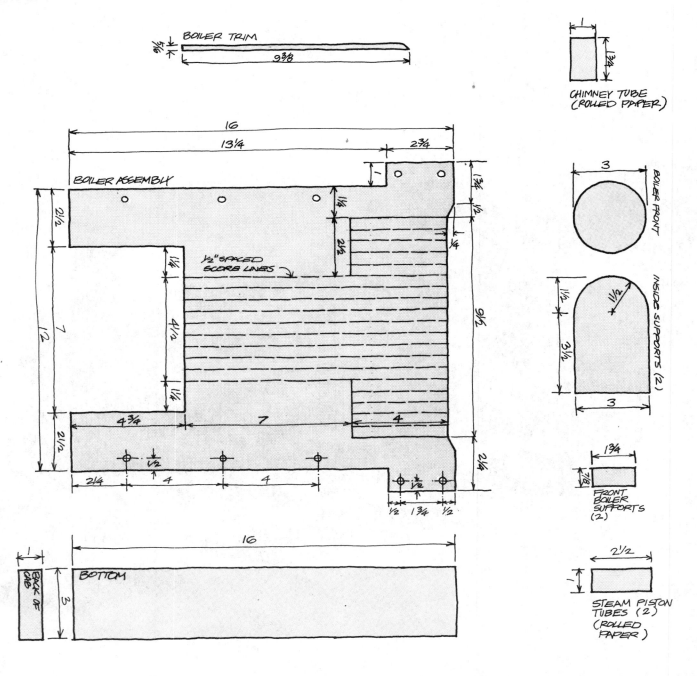

BOILER TRIM
9⅜
³⁄₁₆

CHIMNEY TUBE
(ROLLED PAPER)
1
1¾

16
13¼
2¾

BOILER ASSEMBLY

BOILER FRONT
3

INSIDE SUPPORTS (2)
1½
1½
3½
3

½" SPACED
SCORE LINES

2½
4½
1¼
1¼
7
12
9½
2½
2¼

4¾
7
4

2¼
4
4
½
½
1¾
½
½

FRONT
BOILER
SUPPORTS
(2)
1¾
⅜

16

BOTTOM
1
BACK OF CAB
3

STEAM PISTON
TUBES (2)
(ROLLED
PAPER)
2½
1

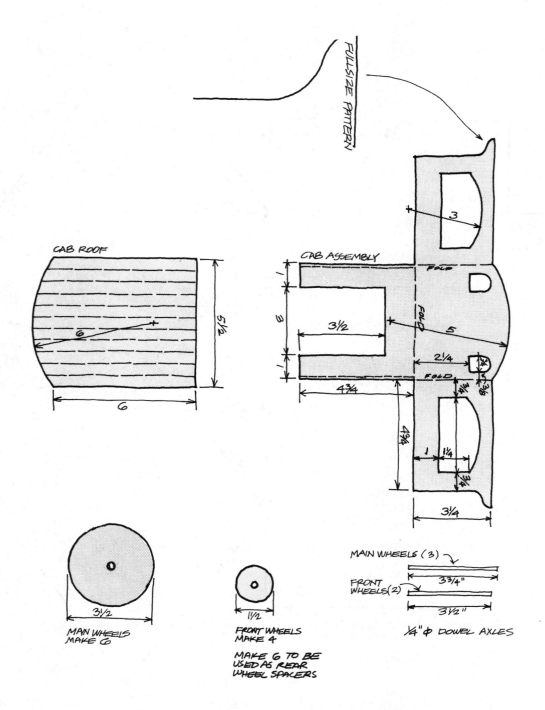

FULLSIZE PATTERN

CAB ROOF

6

5½

6

CAB ASSEMBLY

FOLD

FOLD

FOLD

3

1

6

1

3½

2¼

5

4¾

4¾

1

1¼

3¼

MAIN WHEELS
MAKE 6

3½

FRONT WHEELS
MAKE 4

1½

MAKE 6 TO BE
USED AS REAR
WHEEL SPACERS

MAIN WHEELS (3)

3¾"

FRONT
WHEELS (2)

3½"

¼"⌀ DOWEL AXLES

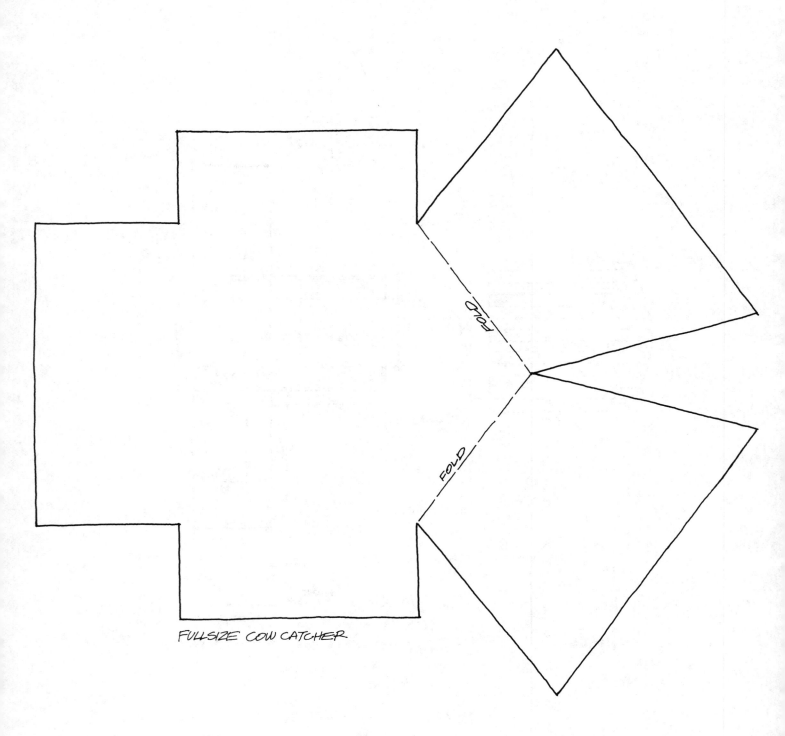

FOLD

FOLD

FULLSIZE COW CATCHER

971

NUMBERS TO TRANSFER

POSTERBOARD
DISCS TO HOLD
PISTONS ON.
MAKE 4 WITH $\frac{1}{4}$"
HOLE PUNCH

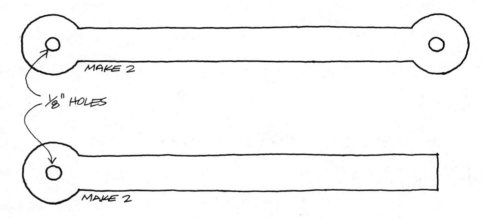

MAKE 2

$\frac{1}{8}$" HOLES

MAKE 2

FULLSIZE PISTON DRIVE PARTS
CUT FROM CHIPBOARD

Assembly

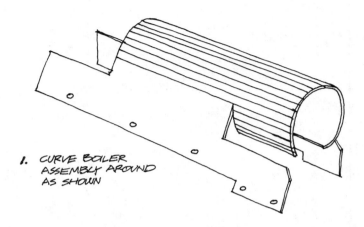

1. CURVE BOILER
ASSEMBLY AROUND
AS SHOWN

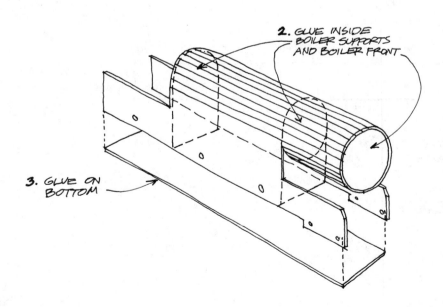

2. GLUE INSIDE
BOILER SUPPORTS
AND BOILER FRONT

3. GLUE ON
BOTTOM

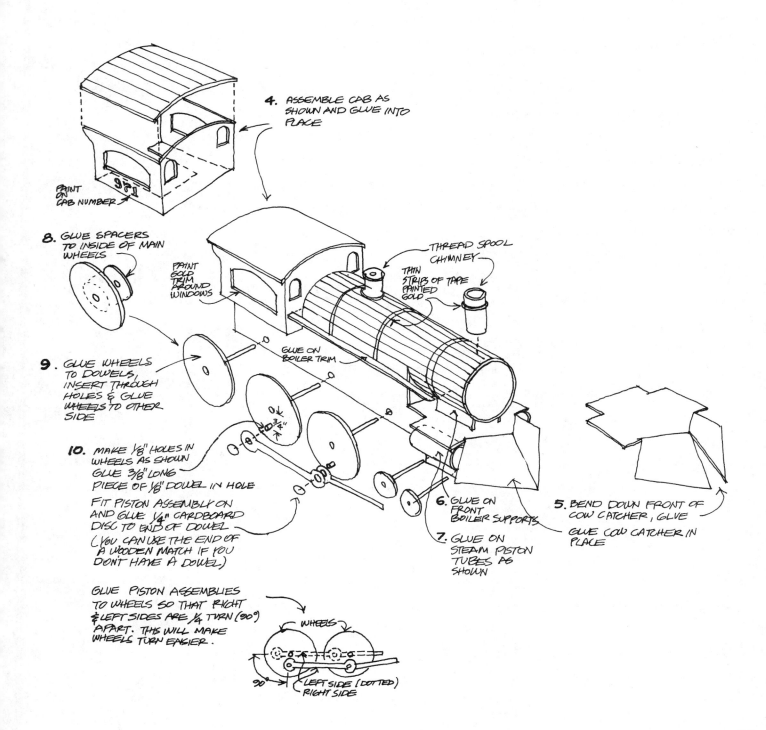

4. ASSEMBLE CAB AS SHOWN AND GLUE INTO PLACE

PAINT ON CAB NUMBER

8. GLUE SPACERS TO INSIDE OF MAIN WHEELS

PAINT GOLD TRIM AROUND WINDOWS

THREAD SPOOL CHIMNEY

THIN STRIP OF TAPE PAINTED GOLD

GLUE ON BOILER TRIM

9. GLUE WHEELS TO DOWELS, INSERT THROUGH HOLES & GLUE WHEELS TO OTHER SIDE

10. MAKE ⅛" HOLES IN WHEELS AS SHOWN GLUE ⅜" LONG PIECE OF ⅛" DOWEL IN HOLE

¾"

FIT PISTON ASSEMBLY ON AND GLUE ¼" CARDBOARD DISC TO END OF DOWEL (YOU CAN USE THE END OF A WOODEN MATCH IF YOU DON'T HAVE A DOWEL)

GLUE PISTON ASSEMBLIES TO WHEELS SO THAT RIGHT & LEFT SIDES ARE ¼ TURN (90°) APART. THIS WILL MAKE WHEELS TURN EASIER.

WHEELS

90°

LEFT SIDE (DOTTED) RIGHT SIDE

6. GLUE ON FRONT BOILER SUPPORTS

7. GLUE ON STEAM PISTON TUBES AS SHOWN

5. BEND DOWN FRONT OF COW CATCHER, GLUE
GLUE COW CATCHER IN PLACE